Morning in the House by the Field

PRINTS

Michelle Gonzalez

ISBN: 979-8-9936595-2-7

Published by: Book Publish Pro

<u>Dedication</u>

To my family and all the families out there taking time to listen, laugh, and share in the memories. May you always feel the love and support.

<u>Acknowledgment</u>

"215/60/91" also appeared Slouching Towards Mt. Rubidoux Manor

"Elegy for My Grandma Who Some Called Abuela" also appeared in The GNU

"I Remember Winter" also appeared in The GNU

"Midnight Drives" also appeared in 2011 Writing from Inlandia

"Spiritual Journey to Mt. Rubidoux" also appeared in 2011 Writing from Inlandia

Table of Contents

Picking the Lot

Morning in the House by the Field

The sun is rising,
and the moon retreats
in opposition with its counterpart.
The distant green field
fills with thick white fog.
The cold wind stirs
the weeds as the dog barks
at the rooster's sharp call.
Just beyond the mist,
sunlight interrupts the darkness.

The cars pull away,
and voices bidding farewell.
All around, workers start their day
with cups of bitter coffee
and bean-and-egg burritos,
just as those before them.
With a quick wave to neighbors,
they all leave for a ten-hour day.

Such is the life of the working man.
Hellos, goodbyes,
and this one house-
rented by a field.

Family Portrait

This is my older brother
in the Ninja Turtle costume.
The neighbor down the street
made it for him,
but you can't see his silly face
or curly brown hair.
My sister is the taller one
with the French Maid costume,
braces and all.
She thinks she looks cute-
but that's just her opinion.
I'm the one with round ears
and a funny-looking tail,
my wavy brown hair
falling to my waist.
There is someone missing-
but it isn't my mom.
She's taking a picture of us,
smiling in front of the old
brown striped couches
in the living room.

We're waiting for our dad.
Maybe he is working,
or is up the street,
drinking with his friends.
It's getting late.
Behind the camera, my mom
grows impatient, yelling at us
to stay still- partly
because we beg to go out
trick-or-treating
to collect what is coming to us.

A Poem for Dad

Years from now,
when the old oak tree in the front yard
is dead or chopped into firewood,
I will still remember
The night you asked
in a drunken voice,
"How will you remember me?"

Maybe for the way you smiled
when mom came home
after she had worked late
on her usual split shift driving busses,
and you had hamburger patties
on the table for all of us to eat.
The food had gone cold
as we begged to eat,
but we had to wait for her.
We fell asleep at the table
and you carried us to bed.

Or the way you showed up
to my 6th grade promotion,
but went back to work
and missed the breakfast afterwards.

That was over 15 years ago
when you were in your 30s,
your cheeks red from your love of beer.
Your insides were shriveled like pickles.
I did not understand why you woke up
every morning and made your lunch

in silence, to go to a job you hated,
waiting for peace that would never come.

Should Not

I should not have leaned over
and kissed him on the forehead
while he was by the sandbox.

Stephannie looked over in amazement,
along with the other girls in the class.

No one believed
what I had just done.

The first girl in third grade
to declare her love,
only to not have
the gesture returned.

Little Boat

My little boat sank
And I could no longer see it
pass over the horizon.

I watched the boats wander by
as I sat on the beach
and imagined I was on one
going somewhere far away.

I lie on my towel in the sand
and fall asleep to the soothing sounds
of the waves crashing
in the ocean.

The next summer, I looked
for my little boat,
but it was gone.

It went somewhere far
without me.

Coming Clean

We carved pumpkins
and decorated the house,
spider webs and all.
I asked my mom
if I could be an angel
just like all the years before.
Something about the halo
and the wings
that felt wonderful
in the wind.

A few years later,
I wanted to be a witch
with a broom and all.
What a wicked feeling,
trading the wings for warts.

Such freedom
to finally feel
like you can be
yourself.

Road to El Paso

We would always leave
after the sun had disappeared.
It would always be
in the middle of summer.

We prepared sandwiches
and other snacks
for the twelve-hour drive.

I remember that after thirty minutes,
I would look out the foggy window
and feel like I was so far away
from home.
I would see nothing but
the black asphalt
and little yellow dots
in front of me,
the sleeping moon
rising above the colorful mountains.

An hour later, we would pass
the wondrous windmills
that always gave me
this eerie feeling.

After that,
there was nothing to see
except the bright stars
you can't see
anywhere else.

Sisters

I'm watching my sister's right hand
holding the neon phone to her ear.
She is talking to one of her friends.
I am not allowed to listen,
so instead, I try to read her lips
as I watch her place her left
hand on her hip.

She is five years older.
We live in different worlds.
I never told her that I envied
the way she was able to curl
her long brown hair
or that I also wanted to be 5'2"
and wear size six jeans.

We share a small room,
but have nothing to talk about.
We certainly don't talk about why
she is not talking to her boyfriend
and has decided to move back home.
Instead, we fight over the remote
control for the TV.

I watch her talk with such enthusiasm,
I can't help but be a little jealous.
When she hangs up, I will not
say a single word. We have lived
like this for many years.
It doesn't seem to bother her.

Behind the Glass

I looked into the tank and saw the turtle's tiny green shell and sad eyes.
He still fits into the palm of my hand, but hates when I pick him up.
I thought to myself, maybe he wants to be free to swim in a pond
somewhere
or maybe bask in the warmth of the sun.
The fluorescent light was bright, and I began to see
what looked like my reflection in the glass.
The turtle then turned and looked into my eyes.
Just then, I felt like he was wondering the same thing about me.
Is she sad? Would she rather be someplace else? What keeps her here?

I took food from the container and reached in the tank.
I took care not to let it bite me, even though it was just a few inches
long.
As I got closer, the turtle first ran away from me,
but as it smelled the food, it came swimming to retrieve its dinner.
Afterwards, it no longer looked sad.

Watching from behind the glass,
I saw a creature that I thought wanted to be free,
but I realized it is content in its small, comfortable space
with plenty to eat.

Lament for Tramp

I never saw a dog so loyal
to the family that took him in
as you, the dog that was meant
for my brother but
became everyone's sidekick.

Our backyard does not remain empty,
but is filled with dogs who
do not live up to the obedience that
you showed every day.

They are not the ones who fasted
when we went on vacation
or howled the whole night through
their first time alone in the backyard.

In your youth, your Springer Spaniel
coat was a beautiful shade of black
with white spots on your ears
and even on your belly.

But the cruel hands of time
Sadly, deprived you of the simple
life you were accustomed to.
You walked around blind in one eye
and limping on your left leg.

Did you see my dad cry silently
as he drove you to the pound?

13

He did it to let you move on
to wherever you were meant to go.

Many years after you have been gone,
you are still missed in the backyard.
You, the protector of our home,
my first friend and companion.

Juarez

She wanted to take
us, her grandchildren,
across the border
to buy us something nice,
like a new shirt.
She asked the saleslady
to translate for us
since we did not speak Spanish
like our cousins could.

When we were done,
we waited nervously
to get back to our parents.
All we would have to say
is that we were U S citizens.

The moment came
and we looked blankly
into the officer's eyes
as he asked our nationality…
we didn't say a word.

An hour later our parents
came and claimed us
as their own.

The only words
my grandmother
could and would say

in English was
I am an American.

Next Door

Danielle's house is filled
with sounds
of pot roast sizzling
in the oven
and grace being said
before dinner.
This happens only
once a year at our house.
Maybe because they have
a big table that seats six
and a nice family room with a TV,
while the five people in my house
squish around a table
made for four.

I stop and take in
the new feeling,
so different from the sounds
of arguing over
who is going to
wash the pile of dishes
or take out the overflowing trash
that has not been taken out.
But that is the home I know,
where the loudest person
wins the fight
and we somehow
wouldn't have it
any other way.

215/60/91

Getting on the 215 to San Bernardino meant
we were going to grandma's house.
Passing the 5th street exit,
then getting off at Baseline
meant I would be
making fresh flour tortillas on Saturday
and walking to St. Anthony's on Sunday.

Going on the 60 meant
a trip to the drive-in movies
right by Rubidoux Mountain
where you can see the truckers pass
on the freeway as they honk their horns.
I climb into bed at 1 am after
trying to stay up for two movies.

The 91 freeway to Riverside meant
possibly going to the mall,
getting new shoes for school
or maybe even a long trip
to the sandy beach.

But at the end of the day,
I was always glad to be home
where I have my new daybed
and flower bed set
that matches my sister's.

Grounded

He said we could play
across the street
at the neighbor's house.
I usually would not have thought
the idea of playing G.I. Joes that exciting,
but somehow
I got stuck there for hours
playing in the backyard
with my brother and his friend.
Before we knew it,
time had flown by
and it was 9 o'clock.
When we entered our house,
our dad and sister
had a look on their face
that I had never seen before.
The yelling and screaming started
and I heard something about
cops looking all over
the neighborhood for us.
I knew we wouldn't be going out for
a long time.
I guess he changed his mind
about us playing.

Building the Foundation

Being Thirteen

The baby's swing makes
a tick-tock sound as
my niece swings away in her sleep
with her head hanging off the cushion.
My eyes open, and I see
Jerry Springer on the bright 12-inch TV…again.
The matching white day beds
take up the rest of the room.
The walls, once covered
with New Kids on the Block,
now display photos of
my sister and her boyfriend.

In my little corner of the room
hangs a Mickey and Minnie poster
with a matching comforter
on my bed.
Her dresser has teenage stickers
even though she has turned 18
while my dresser still has Tinkerbell
and other assorted Disney characters.
What hasn't changed is
the old, ugly, brown carpet or the
dirty off-white walls.
I miss the nets that hung above
our beds that held all our stuffed animals,
the matching flower blankets
and our matching Easter dresses.

Michael

Sitting by the side of the pool
at the picnic,
we were both excited to be
leaving the eighth grade.
I thought about the notes he wrote
telling me that he thought
about me every moment of the day.
Here at Shamel Park is where
I knew we would share
our first kiss.
Hanna said she would tell him
she wanted a picture of us
and when the camera flashed,
she would cue him
to lean in for a kiss.
I could hear his heart pounding
as she raised the camera and
the shutter clicked.

Ryan

There you are, sitting in front of me
as Señora Martin reviews
how to conjugate Spanish verbs.
I begin writing to Jessica about how
I would miss your short blonde hair and soft
brown eyes, as this was the last day of school.

You turn and ask what I am writing on my crinkled
college ruled white paper and I lie.
This goes on for a few minutes
as you draw pictures of smiley faces
on another paper you grabbed out of
your green Jansport backpack.

Finally, you admit to me
that you have known for a while
about my desire to be with you.
The world stops spinning
and all goes quiet
as the words, "let's be friends"
exit your beautiful mouth.
I want to cry, but I don't.
I save that for when I get home.

Sunday School

We knew we should have
been feeling guilty
for missing the morning mass
mentioned the week before,
but somehow, we were not.

As we sat in the
quiet classroom,
usually occupied by
boys and girls in plaid,
we decided to make
use of our time
before the bells
would ring out loud
and the rest of the class
would make their
way to the room.

Laurie started the game of MASH,
deciding who Nick would marry
by simply counting lines
on the wide ruled paper.
Then it turned into
truth or dare,
but no one chose
the latter.

We found out many things
about each other,
like how far Sam
had gone with a girl
and who had experience

with liquor and cigarettes
amongst other things.

I still hope that God
has a short memory.

<u>Putting Up Walls</u>

Ode to the First Job

I can see
Monkey Mash,
Strawberry Cheesecake
And Dirt N' Worms
that sit behind the plastic windows
separating the customer
from the flavor
of their choice.
It's Sunday morning and
I am learning how to
use the cash register.
There are too many items
to memorize;
smoothies, shakes,
even ice cream by the pint,
along with the classics
strawberry, chocolate
and vanilla, to name a few.
I have gained my independence
with a four-and-a-half-hour shift
for minimum wage
and I can buy the old VW
Bug the neighbor is selling,
but first, I have to clean
the huge yogurt machine
and then neatly sweep
the floor, then carefully mop.
When done, I can
clock out and go home,
smelling of 31 flavors
and Mr. Clean.

Fall Is Here

The crisp, cool air blew in
through the bathroom window
as I swiftly stepped out of the shower.
I felt the wild wind on my skin
and then giant goosebumps
began to form on my bare body
from my arms to my legs.

I promptly put on my pants,
longingly leaving behind my shorts.
I traded my sunglasses for a scarf
as I left behind my favorite flip-flops.

Then I remember the fresh feeling of Autumn
as I finally walked out the front door
feeling the fragrant change in the air,
I could tell that Fall is here.

Note from My Boyfriend

I want to tell you something.
I see the way you look at me
or rather, the way you don't.
The other day, I thought I felt you
cringe as I touched your hair
and you held your breath
when I held your hand.
I never wanted someone
who thinks the touch of my beard
feels like porcupine quills.
But I'm not sure how you feel
because you never allow me
to get near you.
I also heard from my sister
you threw the red roses I got you
into the trash compactor.
She heard you tell your friend
how you destroyed them
as if they were a nuisance
that you needed to get rid of.

And I'm also not quite sure
if you are aware of
your fear of public displays
of affection.
I see you look around to see
who is watching when I lean in
to give you a kiss.

So, I'm sitting here waiting
for you to open up to me
like a refrigerator shedding light

upon the hungry person craving
to be satisfied. Any chance
that day will come soon?

Elegy for My Grandma, Who Some Called Abuela

Tacos, coffee, and beans.
Sounds of cooking coming
from the small kitchen.
The smell of pinto beans
frying in the pan
along with chorizo and potatoes.

Her round face smiled as she
made up the guest bed for us,
her grandchildren, who came to El Paso
to see her once a year,
but couldn't speak Spanish to her.

The next day, Sunday,
she dressed up in her fake pearls
with grandpa in his shirt suit.
She made us go to church
where she knelt for two hours.
Later that night,
she sat watching her novelas
while gossiping with my aunt about
the rest of the family.

That summer was the last time I saw Abuela,
but I hope she looks back at our visits
as fondly as I do.
When I smell coffee and beans
I will always think of her.

Midnight Drives

On the third of our many dates,
we drove down the 60 freeway
around the midnight hour
to see the glimmering meteors.
We talked about how
beautiful, the sky would look
once we got to the badlands,
small, but still beautiful.
I imagined it would look like
a brighter version of the moon,
glowing in the darkness
all alone.

We passed the exits with the stores
and other signs of life,
until we reached our destination.
The headlights lead the way
to the dark, hidden spot.

We got out of the car and
sat on his dusty hood.
Looking up, all we saw were
the shadows of clouds
covering the dark sky.
There were no meteors to be seen,
but somehow, that was fine with us.
We decided to stay and talk awhile.
He asked, "Have you ever made a wish,
on a shooting star?"
I lie and say, "No."
It's too early to tell
all my secrets.

I Remember Winter

The clouds form, and they bring in the cold
air, the kind where you can see your breath.
Early in the morning, icicles begin to form
and I defrost my windshield just in time
to drive across the newly frozen ground
as I look up at the mountains covered in snow.

I then recall the ground being covered in snow.
Last year, there was a distinctly different cold
when I walked through the snow on the ground
and then once again, I looked for my breath,
but there was nothing to see this time,
the air no longer had its cloudy form.

The clothes I wore took a different form.
I put on a jacket and boots for the snow.
I would not be caught unprepared this time
or risk catching the dreadful common cold.
I warmed my hands with my breath
for I lost my gloves somewhere on the ground.

The glistening white powder lay on the ground
and I thought, "This is winter at its finest form."
I let a giant sigh with all of my breath
as I looked at the beauty of the snow,
quite forgetting that I was the slightest bit cold.
The season makes me lose track of the time.

I recall this moment as the jolliest time
when he and I made angels in the ground,
then drank cocoa inside away from the cold.
This is when the friendship began to form

between people playing in the snow.
We laughed while taking in a breath.

Running, we completely lost all of our breath
and again lost all sense of space and time.
We were completely covered in the wet snow
that once covered the white frozen ground.
We looked down at the shadows and our form
almost forgetting the winter's blistering cold.

I think of this when I see my cold breath,
thinking of those memories that form time
and the white powder on the ground, snow.

On the Roof

The Next Day

They say that being intimate
is supposed to bring you
closer together, but
all I felt was panic,
my shaky hands
spilling my drink on
her deep red carpet
when she came strutting
Into the room, bra
and panties, black and shiny.
She said it was ok because
her parents were out for the night.
I got the feeling she had
visitors like me before.
When I tried to take off my pants
the buttons on my jeans
slipped between
my fingers, and then she
asked if I brought protection.

Afterwards, I looked at her smoothly
sleeping face, clear
of all the anxieties I felt.
I grabbed my clothes,
left quickly and quietly.
Outside her doorway, I stopped
and caught a glance of the moon.
It was not any different, but I knew
somehow I was supposed to be.
I started my car and drove
away under the immense
limbs of oak and maple arched
like cathedrals, and I felt certain

I had not satisfied her.
What was I suppose to say,
after she told me that everyone
is nervous their first time?
Somewhere between here
and the morning I hope
she will forgive me.

Plunging Solitarily into the Dress Shop

It's June,
so I decide to try on dresses
(It's ok, I have plenty of time.)
Car keys,
purse,
just me.

The Salesperson glances at me
hair pinned up,
tight jeans,
welcoming smile.

I don't look too sure
of what it is
I am doing here.
I mean to turn around,
but just as I turn around,
she asks if
I need any help.

She pulls out dresses
that I can't afford,
which causes a sense of panic
in my chest.

As I turned to the clearance section,
I see a simple white dress…
it's breathtaking.

In a few weeks,
it sets in.
I have officially begun
planning our wedding.

Turning Twenty-Seven

It's such an odd number
if you think about it,
I thought to myself as I looked
in the foggy mirror
after a hot shower.
An age where you wonder
what have I really
accomplished thus far
and what was it that I was
supposed to have done,
perhaps make a difference
in the world somehow.

The only thing I know is what
my mother taught me,
which is to give
until you have nothing left.
So, I put down my phone
and run to the aid of
a loved one again,
leaving my life on hold and
hoping to be on the receiving
side of a favor one day.
I then feel bad for these
selfish thoughts
and wonder if this was
the difference I was supposed
to be making.

Considering Teaching

The idea of it is ridiculous to say the least. Children
running about screaming, hitting and kicking each other
in the classroom, then arguing with them like I
was trying to extract a decaying tooth from
an angry alligator. A grotesque endeavor if there
ever was one. I once walked into the classroom
head held high with a matching smile. I became
the very best actor. I pretended I could write
on the board while watching the class with eyes
on the back of my head. It seemed that the class was
becoming accustomed to the routine. The "starter"
in red marker and vocabulary in blue marker.
For a moment, they would take out their brown
number two pencils and white college-ruled paper
and begin writing down at least the instructions.
Fifteen minutes later, there would be minor chaos.
Pencils flying across the room, boys yelling "retard"
across the room. Every second passed by in what seemed
like hours. At last, the lunch bell rang, and the students
ran out as if they were running with the bulls.

During the Day

Yesterday,
when we were just watching TV,
I did not hear the temptation
that comes in the form of a soothing
glass of a blended lime margarita
with a twist.

But today,
after you had gone to work,
I wanted to drink
until I could not walk without
making a zigzag pattern.

Today,
I wanted to drink until I could not feel
the lump in my throat I get
over feeling so alone
like the pale moon by itself
in the sky.

So I drank until I was somehow
lying on the bed asleep
with my jeans still on.

But when I woke,
I found you there for me,
like how you're always there,
covering me with a blanket,
even though you steal it back
in the middle of the night.

The Heat

Now the heat intensifies
as the temperature rises
just above one hundred and ten
degrees.

The staleness in the air
brings me no relief
as beads of sweat
roll down my forehead.

Outside, the black
pavement catches the sun
as the asphalt melts the
children's shoes
and makes them stick
to the tar on the ground.

In the backyard,
the leaves and fruit
on the trees have
dried out and are
drooping from dehydration.

I long for ice cold lemonade
chilled in the refrigerator.

Then the night brings the whispering
of the mosquitos and
the symphony of the crickets
along with a tiny cool breeze.

I sit on the porch
after the sun is gone
and enjoy the little
bit of relief.
My core temperature cools
as I sit in anticipation
of another mind melting day.

Roses

They remind her of the time
he stayed out all night long
and never called.
She waited all night
wondering if he was
stuck behind bars somewhere
or in another bed.
He came back with daisies
the next day.

They also remind her of the time
he forgot to get her
something for Mother's Day.
As he passed the street vendor
selling long-stem roses,
he bought a dozen,
returning with a smile on his face
as if he had just averted a crisis.

This is why
she gets mildly nauseated
when she sees an assortment
of wild flowers…yet again.
He shows up on the doorstep,
begging her to let him stay.

Going to Calico

Passing the shades of blue
that fill the desert,
the temperature rises
above 90 degrees
at eight in the morning,
even though it is
almost October.

Driving through the Mojave desert,
countless phone lines
distract from the view
of the blue mountains meeting the sky
in the background.

Walking through the ghost town,
I hear unfamiliar words
as the two ladies carry a conversation
in their French tongue.
I wonder why they would travel
so far, just to see a tiny town
that is about to disappear
into the landscape.

Sitting on the bench
trying to avoid heat exhaustion,
I wonder how anyone
dared to call this place home
as I see two freshly sunburnt ladies
walking by while they smile.

Heading home,
I picture people fanning
themselves as they walked
down the main street
happy as can be.

Buried

The swing set where
dad taught us to
pump our legs
is buried at the bottom
of the hill in the backyard,
along with the clubhouse
we once told scary stories in.

Where there was once
an obstacle course in the backyard
leading to make-believe treasure,
there is now dirt filling up the dip
where we had our adventures.
It made way for Mom and Dad
could have a bigger backyard.

The three-foot plastic pool,
where we played Marco Polo is also long gone,
most likely taken to the dump.

And these memories are
all we have of a past
you want to forget.
Perhaps because it reminds you
of growing up too fast,
but somehow I feel
we never grew up,
just old.

At Night

Sometimes I watch you while you sleep.
At three AM,
you breathe so soft.
I put my ear to your mouth
to see if you are alive.

Unlike you,
I sleep with
my mouth wide open,
I drool on the pillow
and snore like a hibernating bear
when you are about
to enter a deep sleep.

Sometimes you gently
kick the bed
when you can't stand
the noise anymore
and I wake.

Unlike you,
I sometimes
sleep on the edge
of the bed,
too afraid to wake
you to ask you to
move over.

Fond Memories of the Field

This is where I stayed out
till seven o'clock one night
waiting for Tony to lean over
and give me my very first kiss.
By the time we got to our homes,
no one believed that all we did
was talk for hours
because neither one of us
could get up the nerve
to make the first move.

I look out my window,
see the field and wonder
if I will have a daughter
that will bring a curious boy
into the field and talk all night long.

Another Night

I watched you again
while you slept.

I wanted to reach over
and touch your curly black hair.

I looked to see
if your thin lips were
formed into a smile.

I wanted to see that smile,
it has been a long time
since you looked happy.

A few minutes later
I started talking to you,
I think I finally had
your undivided attention.

You didn't even argue
when I said
I wanted pancakes
for breakfast.

This is when I tell
you all my secrets,
when you are asleep.

Words for an Empty Nursery

Empty, yet full of boxes
that have yet to be unpacked
since we moved last year.

You say that someday
it will be full with sounds
of laughter, but mostly cries.

Then I say that I'm becoming
even more unsure with
every silent night that passes.

So I keep the door closed
knowing that
I may not open it again.

Strong Roots

What scares her the most
is the idea of staying
in one place for too long.
The idea of coming home
day after day
to the same smile
and the kitchen table.

She wants to be unattached
with no one to tell her
where to go
or what to do.

What scares her friend the most
is spending each night
In a cold bed
with no one to talk to
about the book she just finished
or how she feels overworked
and underpaid.

But late in the middle of the night,
she makes herself content
with her small leaky house
and a tiny garden filled with weeds.
And just for a moment,
she wishes she were not
afraid to be free.

My Stove

My stove wants to cook
fancy elaborate dinners,
but it doesn't know how.

It has a hole at the bottom
right in the center.
Last refugee from the 70s.

It imagines what it is like
to cook a three-layer lasagna
and a dessert as well.

For now, it only knows how
to heat frozen dinners.
Marie Calendar's chicken
is its favorite.

But it still hopes one day
to finally grow up and
get over its fear of cooking.

Teacher

I am a teacher who
spent 18 years in school
and never wanted to leave.

I am a teacher who has
had students who look
older than I do.

I am a teacher who does
not have a classroom
of her own.

I am a teacher who
is always learning from
everyone around her.

and I am a teacher who
sometimes rather be
alone, reading a book.

A Dream

Last night I was a Willow tree.
I don't know why I wasn't
an Oak or a Maple.
My long limbs were
able to give shade
and protection.

I stood tall for the first time
in my life,
able to look down
onto the tops of people's
funny-shaped heads.

I was admired
for my long flowing branches
that look as if they were
raining down from the sky.

The countless rings
around the trunk
gave me the wisdom
of a hundred years.

As I woke,
the memory left a feeling
of completeness in me
that will stay
even after a hundred
more dreams
or dark nights.

Translations

The first time I heard
him speak in Spanish,
I think he was talking
about me on the phone,
convincing his parents
to let him stay out till
one in the morning as he
turned a light shade of pink
from embarrassment.

The second time I heard
him speak in Spanish,
he was telling me that
he loved me, like we were
in a cheesy Spanish novella
"Te quiero mucho me amor"
as we lay on the bed laughing

And last time he spoke
in Spanish, to me, he was
trying to get me to roll my r's
but I refused, smiling
as he put on a long frown.

Now he only speaks Spanish
with his authentic Mexican accent
when he is arguing with his dad
or cursing his lazy boss,
but I miss hearing the words
"Para Siempre."

Spiritual Journey to Mt Rubidoux

Hiking all the way to the cross
is as close as I have ever come
to touching the clouds.
I could hardly feel my feet
as I passed the one-mile mark.
I gasped for air,
but my chest felt like it could not open.
Every few feet, I stopped to rest,
which turned out to be
a mistake, as my legs ached even more.
I sat on the huge grey rock
beneath the cross,
my mind went blank
and I thought of nothing else
but the clear sky and fresh air
on this not-so-smoggy day.
And I know
someday, I will return.

My She-Ra

I remember how my mom would
perfectly curl her bangs
in the bathroom mirror,
then twist her hair into a bun.
She always had gold loop earrings
to go along with her uniform
that made her look like
she was a cop.

Her dark gray button-up shirts
and her creased black pants
with a hole punch that
looked like a gun holster.

My mother still has her old uniforms,
but now she is back to wearing
light blue bus driver shirts.
She no longer feels the need
to twist her hair into a bun
or wear the dark shade
of lipstick and blush,
but she still has the look,
which leads people to believe
she is mean.

Only I know the truth because
I make the same face
and act the same way,
She doesn't even know
all these years
she was my "She-Ra"

Tears

There were 27 names for tears
and there were more than
27 people crying that day...
Tuesday.

There were more than 27 feelings
and I tried to reach back in my
memory to pull out a strand
of thought of my uncle.

That afternoon, my mom recalled
the few minutes before receiving the call
telling her that her brother
had passed away.

It was one of the few times
I did not know what to say
as I thought how I'd rather be
recalling all the names for snow.

The following Friday, there
were even more tears as we
said farewell to a gentle soul.

The man who taught me
how to write my name.

Saint Sally (My Grandma)

Amazing Grace reminds me of
Saint Sally.

She is a saint who walked to
St. Anthony's church every week.

Who hung her clothes out to dry
in the backyard, letting her neighbors
see her whites and linens.

She fought with the ones she loved
the most…that's how you knew she cared.

Saint Sally, who did not leave the house
without curling her hair and putting
on her pink lipstick.

Always the life of the party,
having only a single drink.

Whose telephone dial was always busy,
if she was even home at all.

Who is now in the place she wished to be
and has no regrets.

She is Thunder

She is the thunder
that comes after the lightning
and makes noise after the fact.

She is the thunder
who brings in the gray clouds
that darken the sky.

She is the thunder
that comes and goes quickly,
leaving a path of destruction behind.

She is the thunder that
never says sorry
and is always moving.
She travels by herself.

About the Author

Michelle Gonzalez is a native of Southern California and is the author of a few chapbooks of poetry, including Remnants of a Full Moon and Remiss Revelations. Her work has also appeared in various anthologies such as The GNU Literary Journal, Writing `from Inlandia anthologies, and San Bernardino, Singing. Michelle also teaches in the local school district and is involved in local poetry workshops. She continues to travel with her family and experience the world around her.